UNPLUG

BREATHE

CREATE

A MONTH OF ADDRESSING & SOOTHING YOUR LIMITING BELIEFS THROUGH MEDITATION

Unplug Breathe Create: A Month of Addressing & Soothing Your Limiting Beliefs Through Meditation is a work of my own creation.

The information in this book was correct at the time of publication, and the Author does not assume any liability for loss or damage caused by errors or omissions, again, this is my perspective, opinion, and experience, so it has been written as such.

ISBN - 9798987573877

Cover, Book Design, and Layout by megs thompson, megswrites llc
www.megswrites.com

www.inomniaparatuspublishing.com

"YOU ARE A LIMITED EDITION WITH UNLIMITED POTENTIAL."

—THE UNIVERSE

This journal is part of the UNPLUG BREATHE CREATE series & designed to be used alongside a bespoke guided meditation.

Download this month's meditation using the QR code below:

HOW TO BEST USE THIS JOURNAL & MEDITATION

UNPLUG

The first step to reconnecting with ourselves as creative beings is to unplug & disconnect even temporarily from the countless electronic tethers that keep us firmly held in the world of shoulds & must's.

BREATHE

Take a few deep breaths, paying close attention to the way oxygen moves through your mouth & nose, filling your lungs & reawakening the creative genius locked safely within you, exhaling any fears, hesitations, or doubts that may filter your magic.

CREATE

Release your desire to control, plan & perfect every step & movement you make. Embrace the often wild, messy & chaotic magic that comes with allowing your inner creative to explore & play. Prepare yourself to experience fulfillment & satisfaction in new & creative ways.

DAILY ROUTINE

While moving through your day, begin implementing the use of affirmations. Both habits & beliefs are formed & strengthened through consistent repetition & before you know it your thoughts will become truths.

Included below are powerful affirmations that when paired with your daily tasks & activities, will empower you through this month of finding & claiming your own creative space.

I recommend repeating one or more of these affirmations aloud anytime you find yourself in front of a mirror, washing your hands, or refilling your beverage of choice.

MY CREATIVITY IS UNTETHERED, UNINHIBITED & UNTHREATENED BY LIMITING BELIEFS.

I AM A CONFIDENT BEING WHOLLY & UNAPOLOGETICALLY ME.

MY POTENTIAL IS LIMITLESS.

30-DAY ENERGY TRACKER

When you've completed your daily meditation, make note of a single word or phrase that best describes your energy level in that moment.

Day 1	Day 2	Day 3	Day 4	Day 5
Day 6	Day 7	Day 8	Day 9	Day 10
Day 11	Day 12	Day 13	Day 14	Day 15
Day 16	Day 17	Day 18	Day 19	Day 20
Day 21	Day 22	Day 23	Day 24	Day 25
Day 26	Day 27	Day 28	Day 29	Day 30

DAY 1

Spend a few moments listing some of the limiting beliefs that you found waiting within the space you visited during meditation.

_____

_____

_____

_____

_____

_____

_____

_____

_____

_____

_____

_____

_____

_____

_____

_____

ON A SCALE OF 1-5 WHAT'S YOUR
CURRENT CREATIVITY LEVEL?

DAY 2

Looking back at your journaling from yesterday, what
is it about these beliefs that you feel to be negative
or limiting?

_____

_____

_____

_____

_____

_____

_____

_____

_____

_____

_____

_____

_____

_____

_____

_____

ON A SCALE OF 1-5 WHAT'S YOUR
CURRENT CREATIVITY LEVEL?

DAY 3

Revisiting your journaling from days 1 & 2, how do you feel when you think about these beliefs? Do you experience a sensation within your body when you focus on a certain belief? For example; you may feel a tenseness in your shoulders, or a catch in your throat.

_____

_____

_____

_____

_____

_____

_____

_____

_____

_____

_____

_____

_____

_____

_____

ON A SCALE OF 1-5 WHAT'S YOUR
CURRENT CREATIVITY LEVEL?

DAY 4

How do your current limiting beliefs impact your life?
How do they serve you? How have they protected you
in the past?

ON A SCALE OF 1-5 WHAT'S YOUR
CURRENT CREATIVITY LEVEL?

DAY 5

Where do you believe these limiting beliefs have stemmed from? Perhaps they're something you've held since childhood, a certain work experience, or situation with a close friend. Are you able to hone in on a specific root?

_____

_____

_____

_____

_____

_____

_____

_____

_____

_____

_____

_____

_____

_____

_____

_____

ON A SCALE OF 1-5 WHAT'S YOUR
CURRENT CREATIVITY LEVEL?

DAY 6

Let's get really honest. Do you genuinely see any truth or validity to these limiting beliefs? Do you have tangible evidence to support them or are they based in assumptions you've made about yourself?

_____

_____

_____

_____

_____

_____

_____

_____

_____

_____

_____

_____

_____

_____

_____

_____

_____

ON A SCALE OF 1-5 WHAT'S YOUR
CURRENT CREATIVITY LEVEL?

DAY 7

Where could you see yourself if this belief
disappeared? Dream bigger than feels comfortable.
What crazy huge goals might you be able to achieve if
you woke up tomorrow & these limiting beliefs were
gone? Get as specific as possible.

_____

_____

_____

_____

_____

_____

_____

_____

_____

_____

_____

_____

_____

_____

_____

_____

_____

_____

ON A SCALE OF 1-5 WHAT'S YOUR
CURRENT CREATIVITY LEVEL?

DAY 8

Let's flip those limiting beliefs on their heads. Below, take time to write out your initial limiting beliefs from day 1, along with a positive affirmation that you can replace it with. For example: *I'll never be successful*, can become ***I trust that the Universe is conspiring in my favor every single day***.

ON A SCALE OF 1-5 WHAT'S YOUR
CURRENT CREATIVITY LEVEL?

DAY 9

Spend a few moments today creating a list of 10 reasons why you **ARE** worthy of achieving your biggest dreams.

ON A SCALE OF 1-5 WHAT'S YOUR
CURRENT CREATIVITY LEVEL?

DAY 10

What are you afraid of? Really dig into these fears on a deeper level. For example, your fear may be a lack of money. But upon further introspection, the root fear is actually the instability that comes from being financially depleted.

_____

_____

_____

_____

_____

_____

_____

_____

_____

_____

_____

_____

_____

_____

ON A SCALE OF 1-5 WHAT'S YOUR
CURRENT CREATIVITY LEVEL?

DAY 11

What are you big, hairy, scary goals for the next 6 months? Do you genuinely believe that these goals are attainable? What actions are you taking to manifest these goals? Have you fully committed to your own success?

ON A SCALE OF 1-5 WHAT'S YOUR
CURRENT CREATIVITY LEVEL?

DAY 12

Looking back at the big, hairy, scary goals you outlined yesterday, reframe those goals below as having already come to fruition. For example: In 6 months I want to have signed 5 new authentically aligned clients, becomes, Over the past 6 months I've connected with & signed creative agreements with 5 authentically aligned clients. How does it feel to reframe these goals as facts?

ON A SCALE OF 1-5 WHAT'S YOUR
CURRENT CREATIVITY LEVEL?

DAY 13

Close your eyes. Take 3 deep breaths & ask yourself,
how do I want to explore my creativity today? What
answer do you receive? How comfortable are you with
trusting your intuition to guide your creativity?

ON A SCALE OF 1-5 WHAT'S YOUR
CURRENT CREATIVITY LEVEL?

DAY 14

Spend a few moments visualizing your highest most authentic self. This is the greatest version of yourself that you can imagine. How do you feel? How do you spend your time? Who do you surround yourself with?

_____

_____

_____

_____

_____

_____

_____

_____

_____

_____

_____

_____

_____

_____

_____

ON A SCALE OF 1-5 WHAT'S YOUR
CURRENT CREATIVITY LEVEL?

DAY 15

What are 5 traits that set you apart from others?
Think of things that make you the unique individual
you are. How do these attributes serve you? How do
they limit you?

ON A SCALE OF 1-5 WHAT'S YOUR
CURRENT CREATIVITY LEVEL?

DAY 16

Share some of your limiting beliefs with someone you trust. How do they react? Do they also see these as being truths about who you are? Or, do they see you differently?

_____

_____

_____

_____

_____

_____

_____

_____

_____

_____

_____

_____

_____

_____

_____

_____

_____

_____

_____

_____

ON A SCALE OF 1-5 WHAT'S YOUR
CURRENT CREATIVITY LEVEL?

DAY 17

Write a letter of gratitude from your future self to your present self. Be proud of who you are, the things you've accomplished, and situations you've overcome right now, today & detail how these things have helped you to achieve your dreams.

_____

_____

_____

_____

_____

_____

_____

_____

_____

_____

_____

_____

_____

_____

_____

ON A SCALE OF 1-5 WHAT'S YOUR
CURRENT CREATIVITY LEVEL?

DAY 18

We all have an inner critic, some are more mouthy than others. What kinds of things does your inner critic say?

_____

_____

_____

_____

_____

_____

_____

_____

_____

_____

_____

_____

_____

_____

_____

ON A SCALE OF 1-5 WHAT'S YOUR
CURRENT CREATIVITY LEVEL?

DAY 19

What would you do, if there were no limits or fear of failure?

_____

_____

_____

_____

_____

_____

_____

_____

_____

_____

_____

_____

_____

_____

_____

_____

_____

....

....

_____

_____

....

....

....

_____

_____

....

....

....

_____

_____

....

....

_____

ON A SCALE OF 1-5 WHAT'S YOUR CURRENT CREATIVITY LEVEL?

DAY 20

What drives you to get up every morning? What is your big 'why?' This may vary personally & professionally, although when your 'why' is aligned with your core values it will often carry over into all areas of your life.

ON A SCALE OF 1-5 WHAT'S YOUR
CURRENT CREATIVITY LEVEL?

DAY 21

Write a letter of gratitude from your present self to your ego, thanking them for protecting you from harm but relieving them from their duties. Let them know that their services are no longer required. You've got this!

_____

_____

_____

_____

_____

_____

_____

_____

_____

_____

_____

_____

_____

ON A SCALE OF 1-5 WHAT'S YOUR
CURRENT CREATIVITY LEVEL?

DAY 22

Take a deep breath in, close your eyes & focus on where in your body you feel confidence. Do you feel a glow in your chest, a tingle in your throat, a warmth in your palms, or something else entirely? How does this feel to you? What color is it? Be specific.

ON A SCALE OF 1-5 WHAT'S YOUR
CURRENT CREATIVITY LEVEL?

DAY 23

What does your higher self, living your dream life, believe to be true?

ON A SCALE OF 1-5 WHAT'S YOUR
CURRENT CREATIVITY LEVEL?

DAY 24

Spend a few moments completing the sentences below as many times as possible in the space provided. Then, go back through and read each of your answers aloud to yourself.

I'm building belief in myself by _____
I'm worthy of my dreams because _____
I love & admire_____ about myself.

ON A SCALE OF 1-5 WHAT'S YOUR
CURRENT CREATIVITY LEVEL?

DAY 25

What methods or practices can you use to carry a light of energy & confidence throughout your daily life?

_____

_____

_____

_____

_____

_____

_____

_____

_____

_____

_____

_____

_____

_____

_____

_____

_____

_____

ON A SCALE OF 1-5 WHAT'S YOUR
CURRENT CREATIVITY LEVEL?

DAY 26

When do you feel most creatively confident? Where in your body do you feel this? How would you describe this feeling or sensation? How might you be able to weave this into your daily life?

ON A SCALE OF 1-5 WHAT'S YOUR
CURRENT CREATIVITY LEVEL?

DAY 27

Spend a few moments journaling about the people, things & opportunities you want to attract into your life. There is nothing too small or large.

ON A SCALE OF 1-5 WHAT'S YOUR
CURRENT CREATIVITY LEVEL?

DAY 28

What is standing in your way right now, in this
moment? What might happen if you move past it?
What might happen if you don't?

_____

_____

_____

_____

_____

_____

_____

_____

_____

_____

_____

_____

_____

_____

_____

ON A SCALE OF 1-5 WHAT'S YOUR
CURRENT CREATIVITY LEVEL?

DAY 29

What gifts do you have to give the world?

ON A SCALE OF 1-5 WHAT'S YOUR
CURRENT CREATIVITY LEVEL?

DAY 30

What affirmations are you taking with you into the next week, month, year to replace the limiting beliefs you've overcome?

_____

_____

_____

_____

_____

_____

_____

_____

_____

_____

_____

_____

_____

_____

_____

_____

_____

ON A SCALE OF 1-5 WHAT'S YOUR
CURRENT CREATIVITY LEVEL?

If you already have an
UNPLUG BREATHE CREATE
subscription, keep an eye on your
mailbox for your next delivery.

If you aren't yet a member but
would like to be, or are
interested in gifting a
membership to someone else,
scan the QR code below.

www.ingramcontent.com/pod-product-compliance
Lightning Source LLC
Chambersburg PA
CBHW070448130626
46553CB00006B/2311